It's Catching

Colds

Angela Royston

Designed by David Oakley/Arnos Design
Illustrations by Jeff Edwards
Originated by Dot Gradations
Printed in Hong Kong, China

06 05 04 03 02
10 9 8 7 6 5 4 3 2

Library of Congress Cataloging-in-Publication Data
Royston, Angela.
    Colds / Angela Royston.
        p. cm. -- (It's catching)
    Includes bibliographical references and index.
    ISBN 1-58810-227-0
    1. Cold (Disease)--Juvenile literature. 2. Influenza--Juvenile
literature. [1. Cold (Disease) 2. Influenza. 3. Diseases.]
    I. Title. II. Series.
    [DNLM: 1. Common Cold--Juvenile Literature. 2. Influenza—
Juvenile Literature. WC 510 R892c 2001]

RF361.R69 2001
616.2'03--dc21
                        00-012833

Acknowledgments
The publishers would like to thank the following for permission to reproduce photographs:
p. 26 Claire Paxton/Bubbles; pp. 4, 5, 28, 29 Gareth Boden; p. 10 Ryan McVay/PhotoDisc; Science Photo Library: pp. 7 P. Motta, 8, 9 Linda Stannard, 11 Oscar Burriel, 13, 14 Omikron, 15 Gable Jerrican, 17 Galliard Jerrican, 18 John Greim, 21 Sheila Terry, 23 Brian Yarvin, 24, 25 Geoff Tompkinson; p. 22 Ben Edwards/Stone; Tony Stone: pp. 12 Suzanne and Nick Geary, 16 Vincent Oliver, 19 Elie Bernager, 27 Andy Sacks.

Cover photograph reproduced with permission of James Darell/Stone.

Every effort has been made to contact copyright holders of any material reproduced in this book. Any omissions will be rectified in subsequent printings if notice is given to the Publisher.

Some words are shown in bold, **like this.** You can find out what they mean by looking in the glossary.

Contents

What Are Colds? 4

Healthy Nose and Throat 6

What Causes Colds? 8

How Do You Catch a Cold? 10

First Signs. 12

What Happens Next? 14

Fever 16

Treatment 18

Coughs. 20

Another Illness. 22

Looking for a Cure 24

Staying Healthy 26

Think About It!. 28

Answers 30

Glossary. *31*

More Books to Read *32*

Index. *32*

What Are Colds?

Colds are a type of illness. They affect your nose, **throat,** and often your breathing tubes.

Colds are very **infectious.** This means that if you have a cold you can easily give it to the people around you.

Healthy Nose and Throat

You breathe air into your body through your nose and mouth. The air passes down your **throat** into your breathing tubes and then into your **lungs.**

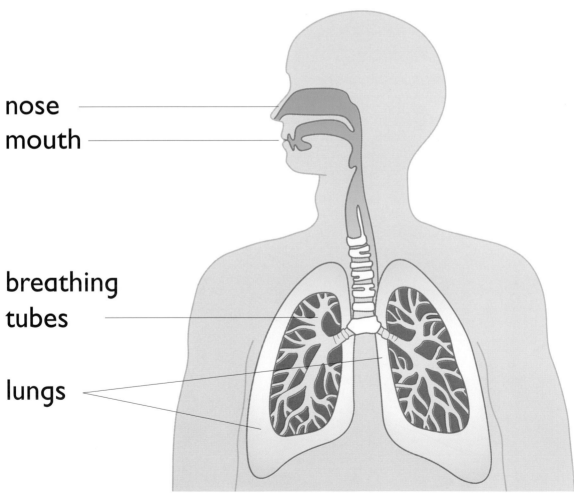

nose

mouth

breathing tubes

lungs

Tiny hairs in the nose and breathing tubes help to catch dirt and **germs** before they reach your lungs. This is what the hairs look like using a **microscope.**

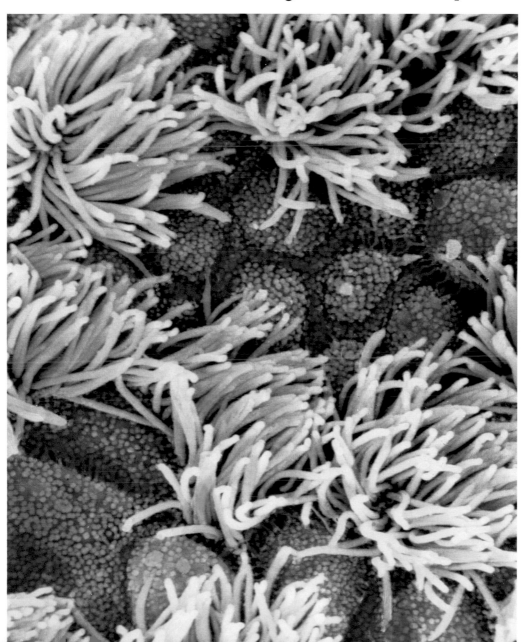

What Causes Colds?

Colds are caused by tiny **germs** called **viruses.** There are several different viruses that cause colds.

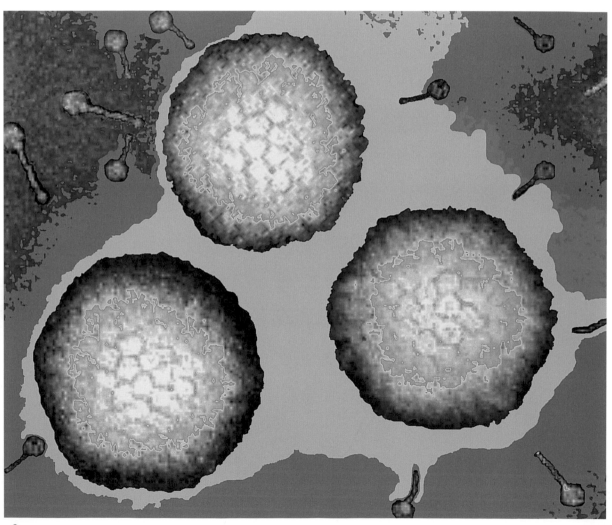

These pictures show two of the viruses through a **microscope.** They have been specially colored to show them more clearly.

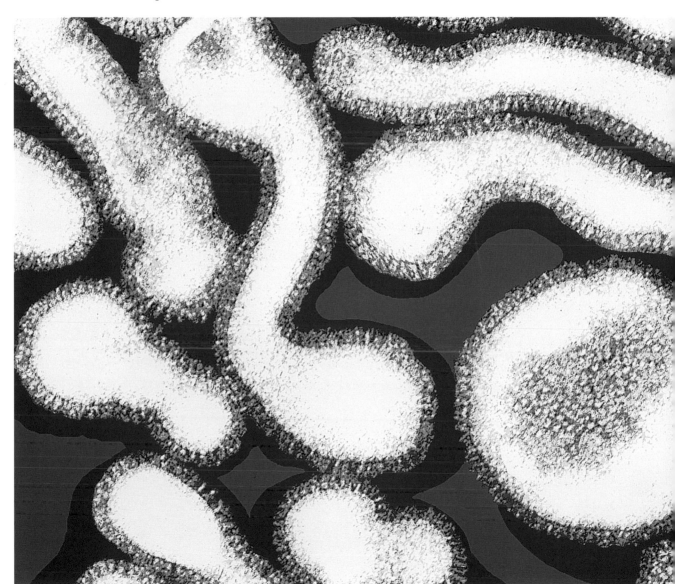

How Do You Catch a Cold?

Every time someone with a **cold** breathes out, lots of tiny **germs** are carried into the air. Anyone nearby could breathe in some of the germs.

The germs may make them sick, too.
Coughing or sneezing pushes out even
more germs—millions of germs every time!

First Signs

The first sign that you have a **cold** could be sneezing, a sore **throat,** or a headache. It could even be all three of these!

When you catch a cold, you will probably feel very sick. You may also feel shivery, and your **muscles** and **joints** may ache.

What Happens Next?

When you have a **cold virus,** special **blood cells** in your body work to kill the virus. These blood cells are colored white in this photo.

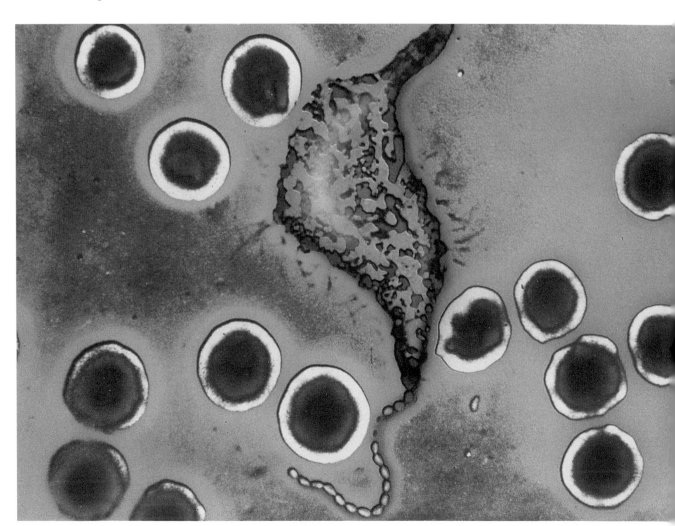

Your body also makes a lot of **mucus** to wash away the viruses. Too much mucus can block your nose or make your nose runny.

Fever

When your body fights a **cold virus,** your **blood** sometimes becomes hotter. This is called a **fever.** A high fever can make you feel very sick.

You may feel cold, but your whole body is hotter than normal. A **thermometer** can be used to measure your **temperature.**

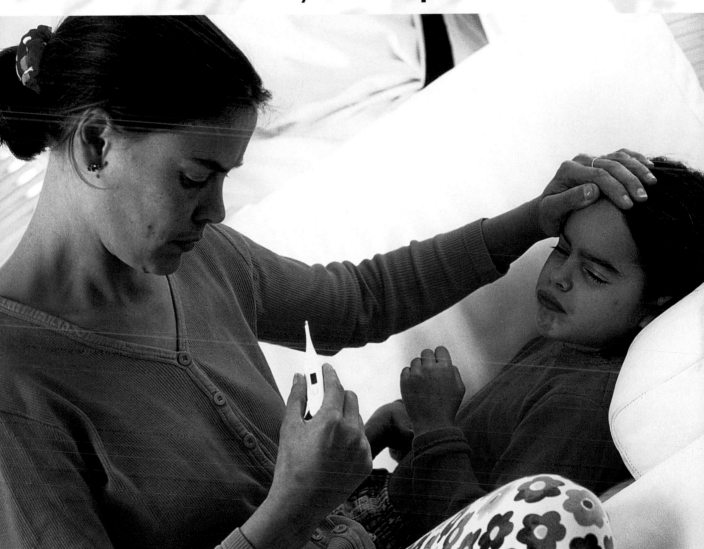

Treatment

There is no **medicine** that will make your **cold** go away more quickly. If you are given a **painkiller,** however, it will help you feel less sick.

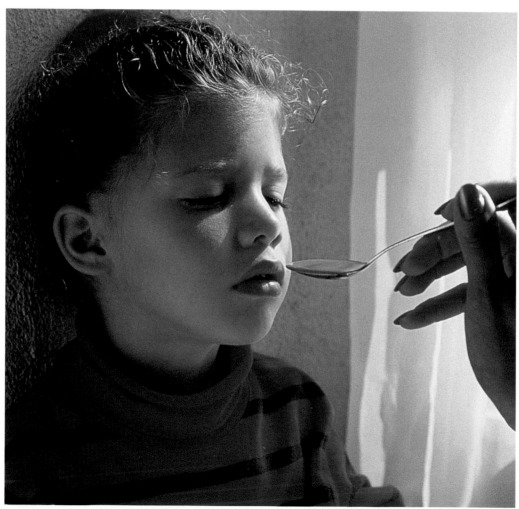

Painkillers help you feel more comfortable, but you should never be given more than the bottle says. Plenty of rest and juice and water will help, too.

Coughs

After seven to ten days you should feel much better. Even when you feel better, the tubes in your chest may still be full of **mucus.**

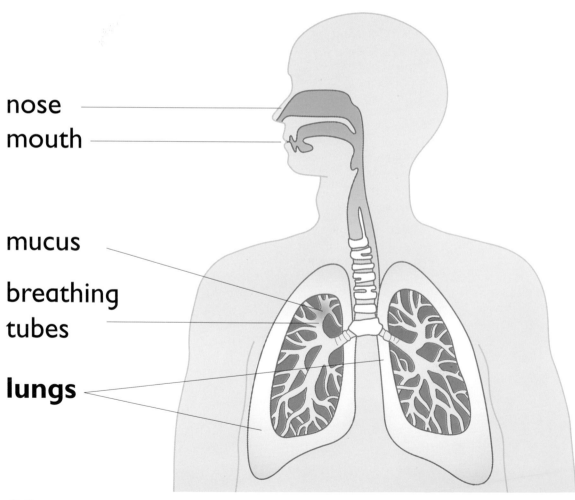

nose

mouth

mucus

breathing tubes

lungs

Coughing helps clear away extra mucus left in your chest. If the cough keeps you from sleeping, an adult can give you some cough **medicine** to **soothe** it.

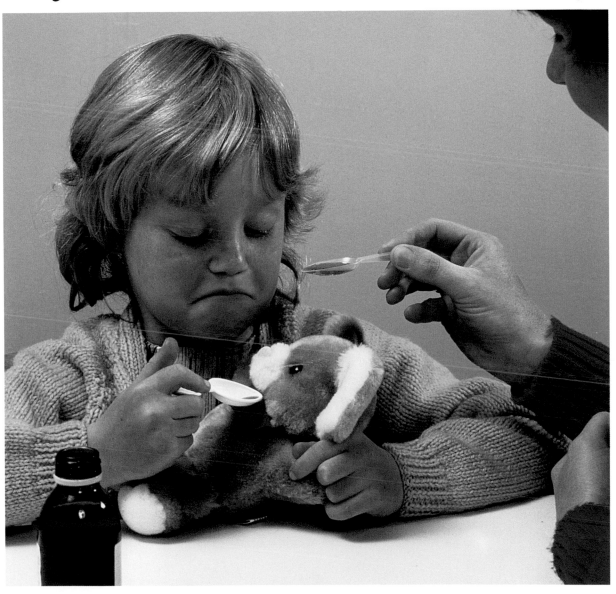

Another Illness

Sometimes a **cold** can lead to another, different illness. If you start coughing up green **mucus,** you may have a chest **infection.**

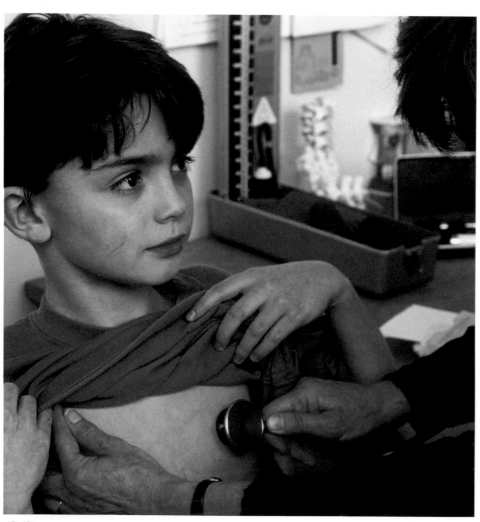

If you get a bad earache, you may have an ear infection. A doctor can give you some **medicine** to make your ear or chest better.

Looking for a Cure

Scientists try to find cures for **colds.**
This is very difficult because there are
so many different cold **viruses**—and
new ones keep appearing!

People can have an **injection** to help fight some viruses, such as **flu.** But there are too many different cold viruses to have an injection that works to fight all of them.

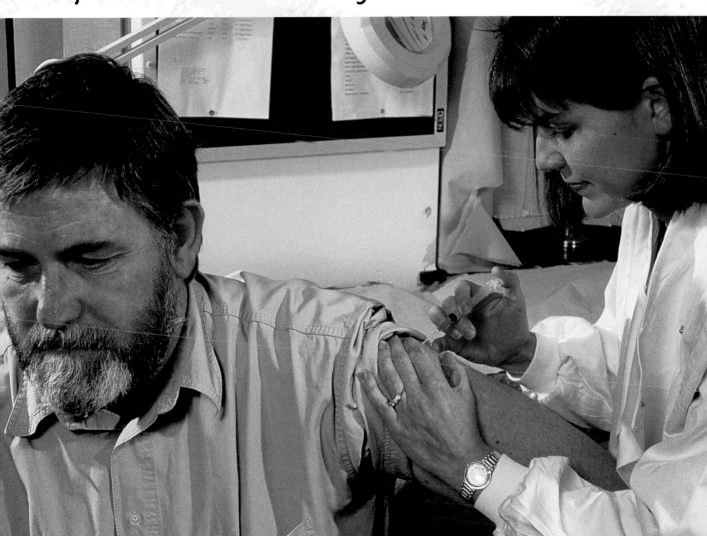

Staying Healthy

Colds are very common illnesses. Eating plenty of fruit and raw vegetables will help your body to fight these **viruses.**

It is important to wash your hands before eating and after using the bathroom. Getting lots of fresh air, exercise, and sleep will also help you stay healthy.

Think About It!

If you have a bad **cold,** should you be brave and go to school, or should you stay at home if you can?*

What can you do to keep other people from catching your cold?*

*Read page 30 to find out.

Answers

Page 28

If you have a bad **cold,** it is better to stay at home if you can. At school you will probably pass the cold on to your friends. You should always stay at home if you have a **fever.**

Page 29

Cover your nose with a tissue when you sneeze. Used paper tissues are full of **germs,** so do not leave them lying around. Throw them away instead. Cover your mouth with your hand when you cough.

Stay Healthy and Safe!

1. Always tell an adult if you feel sick or think there is something wrong with you.

2. Never take any **medicine** or use any **ointment** unless it is given to you by an adult you trust.

3. Remember, the best way to stay healthy and safe is to eat good food, drink lots of water, keep clean, exercise, and get lots of sleep.

Glossary

blood   red liquid that is pumped through your body by your heart

blood cell   tiny building block that forms your blood; your blood has millions of blood cells

cold   illness that usually includes a sore throat, runny nose, and cough

fever   when the temperature of your blood is hotter than usual

flu   virus like a cold with a fever. Flu is short for influenza.

germ   tiny living thing that makes you sick if it gets inside your body

infection   illness caused by germs

infectious   can be passed from one person to another and can make you sick

injection   liquid pushed into the body by a syringe, often to keep you from getting an illness

joint   place where two bones meet

lung   part of your body that takes in oxygen from the air; you have two lungs

medicine   something used to treat or prevent an illness

microscope   something that makes very small things look big enough to see

mucus   thick liquid made by the body to help wash away germs

muscle   part of the body that you use to move your bones; you have many different muscles

ointment   oily cream that often contains medicine and is rubbed onto the skin

painkiller   something that helps keep you from feeling pain

soothe   to take away some of the pain

temperature   measure of how hot or cold something is

thermometer   something that measures temperature

throat   part of the body that joins your mouth to the tubes that lead to your lungs and stomach

virus   tiny living thing that can make you sick if it gets inside your body

Index

aching muscles and joints   13
blood cells   14
breathing tubes   4, 6, 7, 20
catching a cold   5, 10–11, 29
chest infection   22
coughing   11, 20–21, 22, 30
cures   24
dirt   7
earache   23
ear infection   23
fever   16–17, 30
flu   25
germs   7, 8, 10–11, 30
headache   12
healthy life   26–27, 30

infection   5, 22
injections   25
lungs   6, 20
microscope   7, 9
mucus   15, 20, 21, 22
nose   4, 6–7, 15
painkillers   18, 19
shivering   13
signs of a cold   12–13
sneezing   11, 12, 30
temperature   17
thermometer   17
throat   4, 6, 12
treatments   18–19
viruses   8–9, 14, 16, 24, 25, 26

More Books to Read

Hundley, David H. *Viruses*. Vero Beach, Fla.: Rourke Press, 1998.

Royston, Angela. *Clean and Healthy*. Chicago: Heinemann Library, 1999.

Silverstein, Alvin, Virginia B. Silverstein, and Laura S. Nunn. *Common Colds*. Danbury, Conn.: Franklin Watts, 1999.